DRONES AND COMMERCE

MARY-LANE KAMBERG

ROSEN
PUBLISHING

New York

For Kendall

Published in 2017 by The Rosen Publishing Group
29 East 21st Street, New York, NY 10010

Copyright 2017 by The Rosen Publishing Group, Inc.

First Edition   MAY 0 8 2017

Library of Congress Cataloging-in-Publication Data

Names: Kamberg, Mary-Lane, 1948– author.
Title: Drones and commerce / Mary-Lane Kamberg.
Description: First edition. | New York, NY : Rosen Publishing, 2017. | Series: Inside the world of drones | Audience: Grades 7 to 12. | Includes bibliographical references and index.
Identifiers: LCCN 2016029555 | ISBN 9781508173410 (library bound)
Subjects: LCSH: Drone aircraft—United States—Juvenile literature. | Aeronautics, Commercial—United States—Juvenile literature. | Aeronautics, Commercial—Law and legislation—Juvenile literature. | Technological innovations—Juvenile literature.
Classification: LCC UG1242.D7 K36 2017 | DDC 629.133—dc23
LC record available at https://lccn.loc.gov/2016029555

Manufactured in China

CONTENTS

INTRODUCTION

A patient in a remote health center in Rwanda needs a transfusion of type-A blood to survive. The health center is out of blood. In the past, a phone call to a medical supplier meant a long wait for unreliable delivery by motorcycle in this part of the East African countryside with few paved roads. Sometimes the blood wouldn't arrive at all.

Today, however, a text message to Zipline International results in delivery by air in thirty minutes or fewer. The blood arrives in a cardboard box attached to a parachute and dropped from a low altitude by a drone, an unmanned aerial vehicle (UAV). The drone is launched from a site dozens of miles away. The quick delivery time eliminates the need for refrigeration. The system is a partnership between the company and the Rwandan government. It's the first nationwide use of delivery drones in the world.

In Rwanda, these twenty-two-pound (ten-kilogram), custom-built UAVs called Zips can carry up to 3 pounds (1 kg) of blood or medicine and fly up to 75 miles (121 kilometers) on a single battery charge. They're built to withstand wind and rain. A fleet of fifteen UAVs began operation in the summer of 2016 to serve half of Rwanda. The company plans to expand service to the rest of the country by 2017.

For now, cargo is limited to blood and medicine, but that could soon include vaccines, snake bite kits, and other medical supplies. Home delivery may also be possible in the future.

WORLDWIDE, DESIGNERS ARE DEVELOPING PROTOTYPES OF PACKAGE DELIVERY DRONES LIKE THIS MODEL, WHICH WAS CREATED BY GEOPOST, A BRANCH OF THE FRENCH NATIONAL POSTAL SERVICE.

Before long, drones will revolutionize the way businesses operate worldwide. In fact, drones already offer a wide variety of commercial uses that include package delivery, aerial photography for sports broadcasts, real estate marketing, soil sampling, farm field monitoring, and pipeline inspection for the oil and gas industry. Someday, they might even deliver groceries.

Drones can perform important tasks faster, better, cheaper, and with less risk than other methods. For example, farmers who once hired airplanes to survey their fields can now use drones with aerial cameras to do the same job at greatly reduced costs and less environmental impact. The drone's aerial photography will also often deliver a better picture than airplanes flying at higher altitudes.

According to Reuters in 2015, some economic experts predict that drones can produce as much as $14 billion worth of business activity in the United States within three years and $82 billion over the next ten years. According to Mark LaFay in *Drones for Dummies,* the annual growth rate for the consumer drone industry is between fifteen and twenty percent.

CHAPTER 1

FOR THE BIRDS

Y ou might mistake them for birds, model airplanes, space alien UFOs, or giant science fiction insects. Whatever they look like, drones are making their mark on worldwide commerce. They will soon affect the way many businesses operate.

By the strictest definition, a drone is an unmanned aircraft that can fly without a person in control. However, in modern use the term has some other qualifications. One is called line-of-sight. In other words, drones can operate beyond the view of a person at the launch site. Model airplanes aren't drones because the hobbyist who flies them by remote control can always see the aircraft.

Another factor in defining drones is how their guidance systems work. Are the drones operated remotely by a person on the ground? Or are they pre-programmed to arrive at the site of the task, perform the job, and return? And if they are, does that mean there was no human input or control?

WHAT ARE DRONES?

Using the simplest definition, the first drones date to the middle of the nineteenth century. During the Revolutions of 1848 to 1849 in Italy, Franz von Uchatius, an artillery lieutenant in the Austrian army, got the idea to use balloons to send bombs to kill Italian combatants.

On July 12, 1849, the Austrians launched the first attempt into an unfavorable wind. The next month, the Austrians tried again. They sent two hundred pilotless balloons over the city of Venice. Each balloon, which had a diameter of 6.2 yards (5.7 meters), carried thirty-three pounds (15 kg) of explosives with a thirty-minute fuse. Once launched, the balloons had no human control and no targeting system. When the wind changed direction, some exploded over the Austrians themselves. Little damage to Venice resulted, but the bombs did have a psychological effect. The city surrendered two days later.

In the 1930s, the United States military built remotely piloted vehicles (RPVs). An RPV is an unmanned aircraft guided by a human pilot or a piloting system not mounted on the vehicle. The United States used them to train anti-aircraft gunners. The RPVs were later used against Nazi Germany during World War II.

THE FIRST USE OF DRONES WAS FOR TARGET PRACTICE BEFORE WORLD WAR II. HOWEVER, FRENCH SOLDIERS USED HOT-AIR BALLOONS FOR MILITARY USES AS EARLY AS 1794.

An RPV is like the remote controlled (RC) aircraft developed in the 1940s and still used today by model airplane enthusiasts worldwide. An RC is an aerial vehicle operated by a person on the ground using radio signals.

Today's commercial drones are typically called unmanned aerial vehicles (UAVs), navigating without a human pilot onboard. They can be controlled by a human on the ground or a computer system on the aircraft, and with the aid of satellite communications such as the global positioning system (GPS).

Although drones were first developed for military use, they have gained popularity among model airplane and flight hobbyists who use them for fun. But their uses for commerce are just being realized.

HOW DRONES WORK

UAVs come in a wide variety of shapes, sizes, and abilities. Some basic designs include fixed wing planes, helicopters, multicopters, and tilt rotors. A fixed wing drone takes off horizontally and relies on speed and the air moving across the wings to stay aloft. They can cover large areas at speeds as high as thirty-five miles per hour (56 km/h). However, they need constant forward momentum, so they cannot hover in place.

A helicopter drone, which looks just like a helicopter but smaller, uses two rotors (propellers). One creates lift and forward motion. The other controls direction and stability. A helicopter drone can move forward, backward, and side-to-side. And it can hover in place.

Multicopters, also known as multirotors, have more than two rotors—often four. A four-rotor helicopter drone is called a quadcopter. It can hover in one spot for long periods of time. Multicopters can also come with six, eight, ten, or even more rotors. The heavier the drone and any equipment or cargo, the higher the number of rotors needed for takeoff and stability.

Operating a multicopter is easy. The direction of the craft is determined by adjusting each rotor's speed.

In addition to being simple to operate, multicopters are easy to build. These features make them the most popular drones for commercial use.

A fourth type of drone is a tiltrotor. On these drones, the rotors are mounted on top of the craft so it can take off vertically. Then the rotors tilt forward to transfer the job of lifting the drone to the wings. Tiltrotors are not yet available to businesses or individual consumers. However, businesses have been testing prototypes, including one that shipping company DHL tested in the Alps mountains at the German-Austrian border in early 2016, according to *Wired* magazine. The tiltrotor drone

A COMMON COMMERCIAL USE OF DRONES IS FOR AERIAL PHOTOGRAPHY AND VIDEOGRAPHY. FOR OUTDOOR USE, THE CAMERA AND DRONE MUST BE ABLE TO WORK IN ALL TEMPERATURES AND WEATHER.

took off like a helicopter but flew like an airplane, successfully completing test deliveries.

TIGHT SQUEEZE

Depending on the design and computer software, drones can go places "no man has gone before," or at least places too tight for humans to fit into. Drones also go places humans can't or don't want to go because of heights, fall risks, or environmental hazards. Depending on their composition, drones can resist wind and rain. They can be made from fiberglass, carbon fiber, or other composites to make them strong, sturdy, and lightweight. Drones can travel horizontally and vertically. They can hover. Some can take such evasive actions as barrel rolls, steep climbs, or steep dives to avoid collisions with birds, trees, buildings, or other aircraft.

Drone designs can be customized for their intended purposes. And new ideas for their use seem to emerge on a regular basis. New companies are forming to design and manufacture them. And new prototypes are finding their way to commercial use. Some have sensors to collect data. Others have built-in, return-to-home features or GPS trackers so owners can find them if they go down.

EYE IN THE SKY

Among the first to see the potential for drones were photographers and videographers, who saw an immediate

WHAT'S A GIMBAL?

Some drones come with cameras attached. Others are built for use with specific camera types. Attaching a camera to a drone often requires a mounting device called a gimbal. Drones are built for specific types of cameras, which require specific types of gimbals. The devices come with a variety of features, including the ability to keep the camera level and minimize the effects of vibrations. They may also include control of the direction the camera faces or the ability to keep the image stable. As with any aircraft, weight is an important consideration, along with whatever features are needed for the job.

advantage for taking pictures of sporting events. Soon such businesspeople as realtors saw the value of taking birds' eye views of properties and surrounding neighborhoods. So did other commercial ventures. Cameras designed for use with drones made their way to market for both individual consumers and businesses. Some drones come equipped with a camera. For others, cameras can be selected based on the intended use.

For professional aerial photography, several factors need to be considered. Will most of the pictures be still shots or video? Many cameras can do both. However, the camera that emphasizes the kind of photography needed most of the time should be selected.

Consideration also goes to how the photos or videos will be used. If used in printing or publication, the resolution needed will be higher than what's needed for a quick look at something. Resolution is the amount of detail in an image. The higher the resolution, the more information the image holds and the better the picture.

Finally, when and where will the camera be used? Outdoors? Inside? In daylight or low light? If outdoors, the camera and drone need to be able to work in rain, snow, dusty air, or very high or very low temperatures. Cameras exist that work in all of these situations. Some are more specialized than others. For example, thermal-imaging

A DRONE'S CAMERA PROVIDES AERIAL VIEWS FOR SAFETY AND MAINTENANCE INFORMATION ABOUT THE GEOTHERMAL PIPES AT THE HELLISHEIDI POWER STATION IN HENGILL, ICELAND.

cameras can help farmers determine the condition of their crops. The possibilities are limited only by the imagination.

Looking at the big picture, the most concerning stumbling block to commercial drone use in America is the slow process of creating federal low-level air traffic regulations. These regulations cover the use of guidance systems and such safety factors as avoiding midair collisions near airports. The US Congress has charged the Federal Aviation Administration (FAA) with developing rules for commercial drones.

The trouble is technology is moving faster than the government. Companies are developing prototypes for new drones. A prototype is an original model of a machine or other device used as a sample that can be copied or used to create future designs. In some cases, as soon as the FAA issues guidelines, newer prototypes make the regulations obsolete.

CHAPTER 2

OUT OF THE BLUE

I n the science-fiction film *The Hunger Games*, the character Peeta Mellark lay ill, hiding in the forest of the arena. His friend Katniss Everdeen helped out with a special delivery of medicine from one of her sponsors. The medicine arrived, almost instantly, by a small drone that dropped it by parachute to the ailing warrior.

While the aircraft looked a lot like a science fiction device, package delivery by drone is real. It's also the subject of much interest, especially in the field of e-commerce. According to a survey by eDigital Research, one-third of online shoppers liked the idea of drone delivery, especially because it reduced the wait time between ordering and receiving their merchandise. In another survey reported in 2015, Walker Sands Communications found that two-thirds of surveyed Americans expect online merchants to use drones by 2020.

AMAZON'S PRIME AIR

Seattle-based Amazon, the biggest online retailer in the United States, ships millions of packages every week. It's working on plans to use drones to deliver goods to consumers with its Prime Air delivery system.

Using drones could speed up deliveries, as well as lower their shipping costs. According to BidnessEtc.com, Amazon's shipping costs in the third quarter of 2015 increased 11.4 percent. A year earlier, the costs increased 10.4 percent. Even if drones don't bring down costs, Amazon will gain control over the delivery end of its business and minimize conflicts with such shippers as the United Parcel Service (UPS).

Amazon's first drone looks like a small airplane and weighs fifty-five pounds (25 kg). It carries a five-pound (2 kg) package ten miles (16 km) in a half hour without the environmental effects of burning gasoline. The system uses advanced imaging technology and can be programmed with GPS. Amazon hopes to add tracking ability so customers can follow the progress of their packages' flights.

Amazon's technicians want to add more independent in-flight sense-and-avoid technology to avoid collisions with trees or other obstacles. The company used test flights to show their system's safety to the Federal Aviation Administration (FAA). More than six months later, the agency certified

AS SOON AS THE FEDERAL AVIATION ADMINISTRATION FINALIZES RULES FOR UAVS, DRONES MAY REPLACE DELIVERY TRUCKS TO MOVE MERCHANDISE FROM AMAZON FULFILLMENT CENTERS TO CUSTOMERS.

the drone airworthy and approved outdoor test flights. However, by then the drone they certified was outdated. Amazon was already using newer technology.

Amazon is working to design different drone models for use in a variety of places. Ones that fly in cities with high-rise buildings will differ from those used in suburban or rural areas. Deliveries to apartment dwellers pose a challenge, though. The company is considering use of drop-off zones to serve them. Amazon also wants drones for different weather conditions. Drones for a desert, for example, will differ from those used in a rain forest. No matter the type of drone, however, Amazon wants their models to avoid excessive noise.

ROBOTS WITH WHEELS

Google has also expressed interest in automated package delivery using drones and robots. Google's research and development facility, X, is working on Project Wing. It's a centralized system that would use a UAV along with a fleet of robots. The drone in development for this system is designed to travel long distances using only small amounts of energy. It has vertical takeoff and landing capability. However, in flight, it switches to horizontal movement, like an airplane.

In January 2016, the US Patent Office granted a patent for the drone system that drops an order to a robotic box with wheels in a secure location. The UAV and robotic box would communicate using infrared technology. The box, called a mobile delivery receptacle, would then carry the package to a safe drop-off point. From there, a local delivery company could pick up the orders and deliver them to customers.

According to Google representatives, the system would prevent drones from hurting pets or destroying property. The system would also eliminate the risk of theft from customers' front porches. However, Google officials envision using it to deliver goods to remote areas. The company began testing its theories and technology in hard-to-reach parts of Australia.

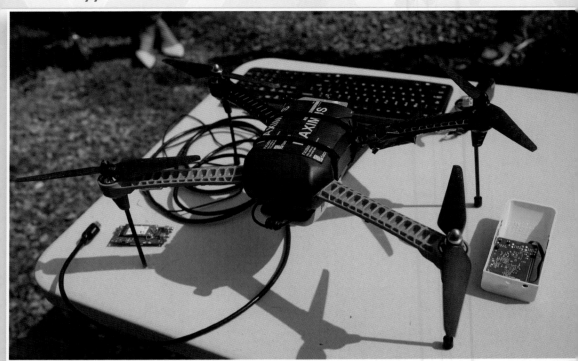

GOOGLE IS INTERESTED IN USING DRONES WITH LOW ALTITUDE TRACKING AND AVOIDANCE SYSTEMS THAT PREVENT MID-AIR COLLISIONS WITH OTHER AIRCRAFT AND OBSTACLES.

REMOTELY POSSIBLE

DHL, a worldwide company based in Germany, is also interested in flying items to remote areas. It has a global presence in more than 220 countries, with services that include domestic and international parcel pickups, deliveries, and returns for businesses and individuals.

DHL conducted long-term field tests of its automated Parcelcopter by taking medical supplies from Norden,

Germany, to Juist Island, 7.5 miles (12 km) away in the North Sea. The trip by the computer-controlled UAV took fifteen minutes each way. The Institute of Flight System Dynamics of the RWTH Aachen University supported the testing.

With government approval, DHL began regular drone service between the northern German town and the island in 2014. The drone was the first officially approved system to operate beyond the visual line of sight of its operator. Not to be left out, other shipping companies, like UPS, and other companies with online offerings, such as Target and J. C. Penney, are showing interest in using drone delivery.

DHL, THE WORLDWIDE PARCEL DELIVERY COMPANY BASED IN GERMANY, HAS TESTED ITS PARCELCOPTER BY DELIVERING MEDICAL SUPPLIES FROM NORDEN, GERMANY, TO JUIST ISLAND IN THE NORTH SEA.

PIE IN THE SKY: DELIVERING THE FUTURE

BASED ON A TEST FLIGHT OF DOMINO'S PIZZA'S DOMICOPTER, IN 2015 IN ENGLAND, PIZZA DELIVERED BY DRONE ARRIVES FASTER, FRESHER, AND HOTTER THAN PIES THAT ARRIVE BY CAR.

Pizza lovers in Guildford, Surrey, England, got a nice surprise early in 2015. Domino's delivered two large pepperoni pizzas using its prototype Domicopter drone on a test flight. The pizzas arrived piping hot faster and fresher than when delivered by car. Surrey lies about 27 miles (43 km) southwest of central London.

The high-tech prototype was flown by remote control. However, if the idea takes off and the chain invests in a fleet of Domicopters, they'll be guided by GPS. The Domicopter flies at an altitude of about 328 feet (100 meters), high above traffic jams, detours, and road construction that could delay deliveries by car.

Restaurant employees cooked the pizza and placed it into a specially designed insulated bag. They simply programed the customer's address into the drone and launched it. The drone delivered the pizza and returned with no need for human control.

A few months earlier, a remote-controlled drone sent off by Williamsburg Pizza in Brooklyn, New York, crashed during a pizza delivery test flight. Later, though, the pizzeria owner launched another drone from the roof of his house. This flight resulted in a successful delivery to a customer—his next-door neighbor!

A GOOD IDEA, BUT . . .

Media coverage has excited consumers about the idea of fast deliveries by drone. However, those in the delivery business who want to use UAVs must deal with several obstacles. The first is investment. While large companies may be able to afford drones, UAVs could strain the budgets of smaller ones.

In addition, e-tailers may have to redesign the way their employees get orders ready for shipment. In current practice, items are taken from the warehouse and gathered together in a staging area where trucks pick them up. The introduction of drone delivery could require a complete overhaul of the process, as well as potentially expensive employee training.

As attractive as the idea of drone delivery is, weight limits and distance limits present hurdles. Heavy orders may need to be divided into several separate shipments, adding cost. It may be difficult, too, for some orders to be delivered long distances. Shippers may still need to use trucks for part of the travel between the warehouse and the consumer. Today's drones travel only relatively short stretches based on battery capacity. However, some manufacturers are experimenting with solar power to increase how far the drones can go without the need for recharging.

Service delays caused by rain, snow, hail, wind, or other inclement weather may inconvenience (and anger) customers and cause the e-tailer to lose money. Other delays and financial losses can result from drones that break or crash on the way to their destinations. Shippers could send a replacement order, but may lose the first order if the broken machinery cannot be found. Finally, thieves can figure out ways to steal merchandise since the drones fly close to the ground.

CHAPTER 3

Down on the Farm

Agriculture is taking on a new look. In the recent past, farmers monitored their fields by walking or using satellites or manned planes or helicopters. These methods took time to perform and time to analyze data collected. Now drones, new software, and new technology offer opportunities to transform agriculture. Farmers already use robots for such farm chores as mowing and plowing. Now they're turning to UAVs for a variety of tasks.

Drones already monitor crops, growing conditions, and livestock. They fly over rows of corn in Iowa, cotton fields in Texas, and almond groves in California. They have been known to herd cattle and chase away deer that are helping themselves to a snack. And the cost of using a drone is

IN CALIFORNIA WINE COUNTRY, A PHANTOM DRONE WITH A GO-PRO CAMERA MONITORS GROWING CONDITIONS IN VINEYARDS, OFFERING A SUBSTITUTE FOR MORE EXPENSIVE AND TIME CONSUMING METHODS .

considerably less than using bigger aircraft.

According to a Bank of America Merrill Lynch Global Research study, estimated growth of the agricultural robot market, including drones, will rise from $817 million in 2013 to $16.3 billion by 2020. Also according to the report, the agricultural drone market may create one hundred thousand jobs and pour $82 billion into the U.S. economy between 2015 and 2025.

And even though getting books, shoes, and pizza delivered by drones sounds exciting, the Association for Unmanned Vehicle Systems International predicts that agricultural use of drones will account for 80 percent of the commercial drone market during the same decade.

PLANTING WITH PRECISION

Gone are the days when farmers planted some seeds, threw on some fertilizer and weed control, and hoped for the best. Today's precision agriculture approach uses sophisticated data analysis to get fields ready for planting in spring, make the most of growing conditions in summer, and analyze soil after fall harvest. The data farmers use often is collected by drones.

With precision agriculture, farmers must survey fields, check plant health, and evaluate crop damage. Specialized software can enable drones to enhance almost any agrilural process. Drones provide everything from a simple bird's-eye view of a field to more complex data analysis that informs management decisions.They can do so in a very narrow fashion, or for thousands of acres.

Using drone technology, farmers can search for and help neutralize such pests as corn borers and learn if vegetation is getting enough water. Growers who produce grains can review crop yield, which is a measurement of the amount of grain produced per unit of land. Crop yield is also called agricultural output. They can study ways topography changes affect output. Farmers can also base their use of pesticides, herbicides, and fertilizer on easy-to-observe facts on the ground. Data collected by drones lets growers identify problems early, before costs to correct them soar. The information can even help them decide when to sell their crops.

A REMOTE CONTROLLED DRONE SPRAYS PESTICIDES ON A FARM IN BOZHOU IN CENTRAL CHINA'S ANHUI PROVINCE. DRONE USE FOR PESTICIDES IS BANNED IN THE UNITED STATES.

THE HEAT IS ON

Aerial maps show color contrast of fields. The maps reveal the true health of crops by analyzing the amount of sunlight the crops absorb. One type of map comes from thermal imaging.

Thermal-imaging cameras add a new dimension to aerial views of agricultural land. Their thermal infrared images are based on the temperature of the subject. On farms, thermal imaging shows how well an irrigation system is working. If plants don't get enough water, they develop

DRONES AS FARMHANDS

Drones can save time and money throughout the planting, growing, and harvest seasons. They gather important information to help farmers make decisions, cut costs, and increase harvests. Mounted with cameras designed not only to take pictures, but also to sense a variety of factors, drones can be used to:

- Inspect barn roofs, silos, and drainage tiles
- Check for irrigation issues
- Evaluate hail damage for insurance claims
- Find missing cattle
- Discover unauthorized hunters
- Perform video checks on lands leased to others
- Modify fertilizer and herbicide applications
- Monitor growing conditions
- Determine soil moisture and temperature
- Check for erosion
- Quantify dry/wet soil patterns
- Determine when to rotate crops or take acreage out of production

water stress and overheat. Over time, the physiology of the plant changes. Crop yield is reduced.

Before aerial thermal imaging was available, farmers used true color and color-infrared aerial photography to identify problems. The trouble was these pictures could alert farmers only after the plant had suffered permanent damage. Now, however, thermal imaging detects issues weeks before symptoms appear on the vegetation. Farmers can take steps to correct problems in time to save their crops. The Vue Pro camera developed by FLIR Systems in Wilsonville, Oregon, records data and also lets farmers see images in real time. The camera was specifically designed for use on drones. Data from thermal cameras is used to analyze plant physiology, schedule irrigation, evaluate plant maturity, and forecast agricultural output. In addition to checking vegetation, thermal sensors can be used to track livestock or unauthorized hunters on private land.

NEARLY RED

GROWERS USE DATA FROM THERMAL IMAGES TO SCHEDULE IRRIGATION, FORECAST CROP YIELD, IDENTIFY PROBLEMS WITH PLANTS, AND TRACK LIVESTOCK.

Near-infrared (NIR) cameras deliver data about soil moisture, crop health, water management, and erosion. They can also count plants. AgEagle Aerial Systems in Neodesha, Kansas, has developed a drone with an NIR camera system.

AgEagle's drone uses three software programs. One flies the drone. The other two record images inflight and process them within minutes upon landing. There's no need to upload them into a ground-based computer. The images are combined for farm management maps depending on the farmer's needs.

To set the UAV in motion, the operator pulls up a Google Earth image of his field and outlines it. The computer then plots the drone's flight path. The AgEagle drone covers a square mile in a half hour. For the best results, flights should take place in full sun or lightly overcast conditions during the two hours before or after noon so the light is even.

Other types of photography helpful in agriculture include red/green/blue (RGB), red-edge (RE), and multi-spectral (multiSPEC 4C) images. RGB data is used for visual inspection of fields, determining elevation, and plant counting. RE data can also be used for plant counting, as well as determining plant health and aiding water management. Multispectral images provide information about all of the above, except plant counting

ADVANCED SYSTEMS

As investment in research and development of UAVs for agricultural use increases, more possibilities present themselves. Event 38 Unmanned Systems, a leading manufacturer of UAVs for commerce based in Akron, Ohio, developed the E386 Agricultural Drone Solution.

It's a fixed-wing drone that comes with a cloud-based Drone Data Management System, along with ten apps that collect detailed information for analysis. The system stores, shares, and analyzes data. After analysis, the system creates maps that can be viewed on a computer or a mobile device, as well as shared or downloaded. A single flight of the E386 lasts up to an hour and fifteen minutes and covers 750 acres (303.5 hectares).

WHAT GOOD ARE DRONES?

Using drones helps growers grow more, better, and healthier crops. Aerial surveillance by drones identifies such problems as pests, heat stress, or mechanical problems with irrigation systems early. If discovered early, the cost to fix problems is lower, and the crop yield is higher.

Scouting crops takes time—especially if farmers try to inspect their land on foot. Drones with the proper cameras and other software can cover large areas faster and deliver more detailed data and analysis. So drones save time and collect more usable data.

Using drones saves money. The cost of investing in a drone system can be recouped in about a year. From then on, the farmer owns the system that will continue to help him or her make operations more efficient and increase crop yield. And once a UAV system is set up, it's easy to operate. Best of all, the drone finds its own way home when its work is done.

CHAPTER 4

WORKING IN THE MINES

Every day at some mining sites, surveyors walk the area. They look for landscape changes that affect operations. The job is dangerous. The terrain often is unstable. Large machines are at work. And the surveyor must walk close to tailings ponds full of potentially toxic elements. A tailings pond, also called a tailings impoundment area, is a wet storage area for particles and chemicals left over from mining. A pond area is dammed up and filled with water to cover the mining waste. It's a place no one wants to get close to.

The good news is that UAVs can do the job—and many others—from the air faster and at lower cost and more safely than traditional methods. Aerial mapping can use satellites (that depend on a clear day) or conventional aircraft. However, drones fly at lower altitudes. That means more detailed data. Drone technology delivers live images with analysis in about a month, compared to satellite images that may be out of date when they arrive. UAVs replace traditional surveying techniques that once took days or weeks. The same information is now available within hours. Timely information leads to better management decisions.

SHOW ME THE MONEY

Drones also cut costs. According to the US Geological Survey (USGS), mapping using drones costs about 10 percent of what maps created with views from a rented helicopter does. So, for example, if it costs $2,500 per hour to rent a helicopter, a drone can do the same job for less than $250 per hour. Using drones is cost effective. Mining companies need only a few months for the purchase cost to equal the savings compared with other methods.

Pilot projects by the US Geological Survey have used

USING DRONES TO SCOUT TERRAIN AT MINES SAVES MONEY COMPARED TO USING MANNED VEHICLES. OPEN PIT MINES LIKE THIS ONE EXTRACT MINERALS FROM THE SURFACE.

UAVs to find forgotten mine entrances, which pose major hazards. Horizontal mine openings, called adits, can cave in. That's because the weathered rock at the entrance weakens over time. Even walking or talking near them causes small vibrations that trigger collapse. It's much safer to send in a drone than a human.

In other USGS projects, UAVs were used to find coal seam fires in Montana, Colorado, and West Virginia. Coal seam fires occur underground, usually in coal mines. Even after flames ignited by human or natural causes go out on the surface, coal deposits smolder for years, decades, centuries, and longer.

Coal seam fires are so common that thousands of them are currently burning worldwide. They're difficult and expensive to put out. They often burn until the fuel is consumed or the fire reaches a permanent ground water table. At any time, they can flare up and start forest fires or light up nearby brush. Toxic fumes from coal seam fires release mercury and carbon dioxide into the atmosphere.

SCOUTING TERRAIN

Mines need accurate day-to-day information about the land they're working on and in. With open pit mines, for example, knowing how much material has moved each day is important.

Mining operations also need models of the ground surface before and after they build their mines. Drones deliver precise blueprints used to make these terrain models.

And drones collect information in a less intrusive way than lower-tech methods. When the maps indicate places of interest, rocks can be tested by digging huge trenches with excavating machines. The trenches must later be filled back in. However, the maps that drone systems produce are so exact miners can use a geoprobe instead. A geoprobe is a machine that drives steel rods into the ground to aid in taking samples below the surface.

When new mines get permits to begin operations, the mining companies must already know how they will restore the land when the mine closes. Under federal regulations, they must return the land to a natural state or a state suitable

EVEN BEFORE NEW MINES OPEN, MINE OPERATORS MUST PROVIDE A PLAN TO RESTORE THE AREA OR MAKE IT SUITABLE FOR INDUSTRIAL USE WHEN THE MINES CLOSE.

for economic endeavors. Mining companies either restore landscapes and ecosystems or create space for industrial or municipal use. Commercial drones can monitor and record the process from the air, as well as conduct environmental assessments.

IN SEARCH OF MINERALS

Drones can do many more jobs, often in more environmentally friendly ways than traditional methods. Drone systems use aerial photography mixed with high-tech software to collect data used to search for minerals, monitor terrain on a daily basis, and aid in long-term planning. Operators use multispectral imagery to find bodies of ore. Multispectral imagery goes beyond the red, green, and blue bands used in other photography. It's used to identify rock's composition.

A spectral signature is a measure of the electromagnetic energy from the sun that is reflected from an object compared with the amount of electromagnetic energy striking the object. Scientists use the measurement to find out what the object is made of.

A spectral signature is like a DNA report or a fingerprint. Different ores have different ones. The one for gold, for example, differs from silver. Silver differs from diamonds. Spectral signatures also show the differences among such other minerals as iron, copper, phosphate, and zinc. Maps created using spectral signatures help mining companies decide where to explore.

TOOLS OF THE TRADE

The United States lags behind other countries in using drones. However, Canada has been using them for years in both the wilderness and close to cities. Drones' versatility makes them important tools for the mining industry. Consider the following two Canadian companies that are using drones for mining.

Harrier Aerial Surveys, a company based in Nelson, British Columbia, Canada, has used the SteadiDrone QU4D, a drone system developed in Knysa, South Africa. The SteadiDrone Qu4d quadcopter weighs just 3.3 pounds (1.5 kg) and has a diagonal width of 25.6 inches (65 cm). Its high-resolution camera mounts in the center for greater stability.

With a fifteen-minute flight time, the SteadiDrone Qu4d takes overlapping photos for mapping. Or, with a gimbal on the front, it can get in close to take pictures. It travels up and down as well as sideways, and it can hover, allowing it to get into tighter spots than fixed-wing drones. It can also take a look at areas where height or environmental hazards pose risk for humans. Using the UAV also avoids expensive operational shutdowns for inspections.

Another Canadian company, GroundTruth Exploration, based in Dawson City, Yukon, Canada, uses the eBee drone, an easy-to-use professional mapping drone from sense-FLY, based in Switzerland. It includes a camera that gathers high-resolution images, along with digital elevation data.

THE QU4D AERIAL DRONE FROM STEADIDRONE, BASED IN KNYSA, SOUTH AFRICA, IS WELL SUITED FOR USE AT MINING OPERATIONS WITHOUT HAVING TO SHUT DOWN PRODUCTION FOR INSPECTIONS.

The eBee is a fixed-wing UAV with a 31.5-inch (80 cm) wingspan. It weighs 1.5 pounds (.7 kg). It flies up to fifty minutes at a time at an altitude of 328 feet (100 meters). It covers 4.6 square miles (12 square kilometers) in a single flight at speeds of 25 to 56 miles per hour (40 to 90 kilometers per hour). The eBee can fly at high mountain elevations and in adversely cold conditions, such as in the winter, as well as in rainy weather, or duirng moderatly windy conditions. Onboard sensors prevent collisions with obstacles.

CHAPTER 5

WHAT ELSE CAN DRONES DO?

UAVs are airborne data collectors. Commercial uses for them are limited only by the imagination. If you can think of it, drones can likely do it. In the field of professional aerial photography alone, UAVs offer almost infinite opportunities. Because the images are taken close to the ground, they come out crisp and clear, with good detail.

Professionals use drones for photography, videography, and cinematography. Some produce images for movies and documentaries. Others provide live reporting of news and traffic conditions. They also take video of football games and other sports for broadcast.

In the fields of advertising and marketing, drones add new dimensions to promotions. Tourism companies offer virtual tours of resorts and golf courses. Wedding photographers take aerial shots of ceremonies and receptions. Realtors for commercial and residential properties promote their listings

DRONES ARE USED IN FILM FOR BOTH VIDEOGRAPHY AND POST-PRODUCTION. THIS ONE IS BEING USED TO PREVIEW CAMERA EFFECTS AT TECHNICOLOR RESEARCH AND DEVELOPMENT IN CESSON-SEVIGNE, FRANCE.

by showing 360-degree shots of home and building exteriors, as well as quick scans of the neighborhoods and surrounding areas.

SNAP DECISIONS

Several commercial drones for professional photographers are available on the market. One is the DJI Inspire 1 quadcopter. Its three-axis gimbal mounts a camera with 4K resolution. The 4K refers to the number of pixels in the image. A 4K camera delivers 4,000 pixels. This is the standard for cinematography. It takes still shots as well as video, and videos can be transferred to a mobile device.

The drone itself has retractable arms, so photographers can get shots with a 360-degree, unobstructed view. Its eighteen-minute flight time disqualifies it for long jobs. But the technology offers stable movement indoors with quick response controls. The drone comes with dual transmitter controls. One person can fly the drone, while another operates the camera. Available software lets users create autopilot, flight telemetry, and manual camera controls if connected to a USB device with an internet connection.

THE DJI INSPIRE 1 QUADCOPTER DRONE WITH A THREE-AXIS GIMBAL AND CAMERA HAS RETRACTABLE ARMS TO ALLOW A 360-DEGREE VIEW USEFUL IN CINEMATOGRAPHY.

Another commercial drone suitable for professional photography is the Walkera Tali H500. It combines the recording capability for professional-quality photos and videos with easy maneuverability. It, too, has a three-axis gimbal that allows the photographer to pan, tilt, and roll. The gimbal mounts a GoPro HERO action camera (not included). The drone has six rotors for more power than a quadcopter. Therefore, it can lift more weight and fly longer—up to twenty-five minutes per flight. Its flight control system offers six choices, from completely automated GPS assistance to manual control. The video transmitter on the drone sends a video feed from the camera to the ground. It also has auto-cruise and return-to-home functions.

CONNECTING THE WORLD

Drones deliver more than pretty pictures. One use is connecting the world. Mark Zuckerberg, cofounder, chairman, and chief executive of Facebook, wants the social networking website to become an airborne internet service provider. And he plans to use UAV technology. In July 2015, Zuckerberg announced completion of the Aquila, Facebook's full-scale, unmanned aircraft. He wants to use it to bring Wi-Fi internet to remote parts of the world. The system delivers data at ten gigabits per second. The UAV connects to lasers on the ground. Because of this, connections may be slower on rainy or cloudy days.

Aquila has a narrow V shape with the wingspan of a jumbo jet. However, it weighs only between 880 and 1,000 pounds (399–454 kg). It's built from a layer of foam inside two outer layers of material made from lightweight carbon fiber.

The UAV uses solar power to stay aloft for three months at a time, circling the area it serves on the ground. Aquila flies at an altitude between 60,000 and 90,000 feet (18,288–27,432 m), higher than commercial aircraft.

IF YOU BUILD IT . . .

In the construction industry, drone systems photograph entire building sites from the air and perform land surveys. Their data collection can be used in planning stages to decide how easily or conveniently a project can be built. They can identify potential problems while construction is still in the planning stages—before costly repairs or changes are needed. As building continues, drone systems monitor the process and aid quality-control functions. Once the building is completed, views can be used to promote and advertise it.

Utilities can use drones to inspect power lines, substations, radio towers, and cell towers. They can also examine power lines, water lines, and wind turbines. And they can detect solar panel outages. Other businesses can use UAVs to check out building roofs for heat and leaks or to conduct surveys to determine maintenance needs.

In the oil and gas industries, drones can track oil spills and evaluate environmental conditions. They can fly over oil

WHAT'S GOOD FOR THE GOOSE

Doing what geese do, a flock of them in a park or along a beach leaves large quantities of undesirable droppings where citizens want to play. To solve the problem at a beach on Petrie Island, city officials in Ottawa, Ontario, Canada, hired a commercial drone operator as a so-called Goose Buster.

In a pilot project, the tech expert built his own helicopter drone with six rotors. He used it to scare away the Canada geese. When the geese waddled around certain parts of the lakeshore, he sent his drone lunging at them like a predator hawk. The geese hurried into the water and swam away.

After just a short time, he succeeded in moving the birds along to other locations. They stayed away from Petrie Island. If the process continues to work, the city hopes to expand the use of Goose Busters at other beaches.This may be merely the tip of the iceberg when it comes to drones effecting change in the natural environment by interacting with animals and other living things. Most importantly, such applications may be minimally invasive, or at least far less so than previous methods.

and gas pipelines to monitor them in a few hours instead of the week it would take technicians on land.

Private security firms use drones for ground surveillance in real time. They can also watch for plant safety and security both inside and outside the business. Walmart has already asked the FAA for permission to test outdoor

IN MARCH 2016, FOOTWEAR PRODUCER CROCS, INC., OPENED A TEMPO-
RARY STORE IN TOKYO, JAPAN, TO DEMONSTRATE HOW DRONES WOULD
FETCH ORDERS FOR CUSTOMERS IN THE FUTURE.

drones with surveillance equipment. The discount store
chain hopes to investigate the use of drone technology to
manage their inventory and supply chain. Drones might be
able to close the shipping gap by providing quick deliveries
to retail outlets.

Other uses of drone technology for commerce include:

- Thermal conveyor belt inspection
- Extraction of raw materials
- Quick delivery of spare parts, tools, and lubricants

- Taking soil samples
- Storm damage assessment
- Evaluation of data before and after blasting
- Video proof of compliance with laws and regulations

DRONE DANGERS

In spite of the ability to perform many jobs that save time and money, drone use has a down side. The most critical is the potential for interference with full-size aircraft, especially near airports. Incidents have already occurred at New York's LaGuardia, Los Angeles International, and Dallas's Love Field, as well as other airports in London, England, and Warsaw, Poland.

A collision between an airliner and a small flying object (even a bird) most likely damages the larger one. It could have fatal results. Damage depends on air speed and the motion of the airliner. If a drone gets sucked into an engine, it can damage the turning blades inside. The faster the airliner's speed, the worse the harm. A drone that hits a cockpit windshield inflight could break it, which can easily cause a crash.

Finally, drones threaten people's safety on the ground in such emergencies as fires. Because of the risk of collision with drones, fire-fighting aircraft have been grounded and unable to reach the scenes of car and forest fires. Thus, they not only endanger aircraft operators but also victims who are waiting for help on the ground.

CHAPTER 6

LEGAL ISSUES SURROUNDING DRONES

The risk of deadly accidents is one reason the federal government wants to develop regulations for drone use. Even so, rules can be broken. In some cases, drones flown by unwise amateurs have interfered with fire-fighting aircraft even though the Federal Aviation Administration (FAA) had closed the airspace near the fire.

The FAA limits UAVs to an altitude of 400 feet (122 m). It also bans them from flying within five miles of an airport. Still, at the end of 2015, the FAA was getting more than one hundred monthly reports of drones endangering aircraft. And according to Bard College's Center for the Study of the Drone in Annandale-on-Hudson, New York, a survey of airplane pilots reported in December 2015 that they have had to veer off course to avoid collisions with drones at least twenty-eight times.

According to FAA estimates, approximately 1.6 million drones were sold in the United States in 2015—many to amateur hobbyists. Clearly, something had to be done to keep America's skies safe. The FAA looked for a way to identify—and possibly prosecute—drone owners in such cases. The agency required registration for all drones weighing .55 pounds to 55 pounds (.25 to 25 kg). Before their first outdoor flights, drones must be marked with these registration numbers. Drone owners older than age twelve must register as pilots on an FAA website. Parents must register children younger than that. To register, the owners must give their name and home and email addresses. Identities are checked before approval.

NASA and Mojave, California-based Scaled Composites worked together to develop collision avoidance systems to keep manned aircraft safe from UAVs.

Registration lasts three years and must be renewed. It helps identify owners of wayward drones. It also gives the FAA a chance to teach owners safe practices. The new pilots learn to fly safely and responsibly according to rules made for them.

STUMBLING BLOCKS

The biggest obstacles for commercial use of drones in the United States have been a lack of clear regulations and the slow process of developing them. That slow speed angers and frustrates such businesses as Amazon. That's because technology is advancing too quickly for the FAA to keep up. In Japan, Brazil, France, the United Kingdom, Canada, and Australia, governments have imposed much looser guidelines than in the United States. Consequently, industry observers say that commercial drone use in those places is flourishing.

At first, the FAA banned all commercial use of drones in the United States. Its main concerns with industrial use were flight altitude, whether to allow flights after dark, and whether to allow flights beyond the operator's field of vision. The early framework for drone regulation came in 2011, when the FAA assigned airspace between 200 and 500 feet (61–152 m) to drones. The agency recommended that UAV use on farms be restricted to less than 400 feet (122 m). However, in 2014 a court ruled that the recommendation was just that—a policy statement,

DRONES FLYING NEAR AIRPORTS CAN BE DEADLY. THAT'S ONE REASON THE FAA IMPOSES RESTRICTIONS ON ALTITUDES AND OTHER OPERATIONS OF UAVS.

not an actual regulation. FAA regulations proposed in March 2015 would allow most commercial drone flights. However, the rules were still too strict to make package delivery practical.

In 2015, the FAA said businesses could ask the agency for approval to use drones in specific areas on a case-by-case basis. The authority for the move is known as Section 333. The process is slow. A business files a petition for exemption, asking to be allowed to use drones commercially. But high volume of requests delays review.

FAA SECTION 333

According to the FAA, all aircraft used in the national airspace must be registered and have a certificate of airworthiness. They also need a licensed pilot and FAA approval to operate.

Section 333 of the FAA Modernization and Reform Act of 2012 gives the secretary of transportation the authority over UAVs. A business can ask for an exemption or authorization to be free from the rule. In practice, the business files a petition to the government asking that the rules be waived. The secretary reviews the petition and makes a decision one case at a time. Once the FAA completes its rules for small UAV operations, businesses will know which rules they must follow and won't need to file for special status.

And not every applicant wins permission. According to the FAA, as of April 18, 2016, however, the agency had granted 4,888 requests. The approvals come with conditions and limitations that operators must follow.

In 2015, regulators also allowed drone use for agricultural purposes throughout the growing season. The FAA recognized that drones used in large rural areas lack most of the privacy and safety concerns that arise in more heavily populated suburbs and cities.

Some FAA regulations for commercial drones were expected to be completed in 2016. However, these will likely cover only simple systems. They won't include flights at altitudes higher than 500 feet (152 m) or beyond the operator's sight. The agency is also still a long way from drafting rules for automated package delivery. Meanwhile the ban on use of drones for business purposes remains. Until then, companies like Amazon will have to take their business elsewhere, to other potential markets. The FAA's work on complete rules for drones in the United States will likely take until at least 2019.

TIRED OF DELAYS

On May 13, 2015, two US senators got tired of waiting. Cory Booker, a Democrat from New Jersey, and John Hoeven, a Republican from North Dakota, introduced a bill to set UAV guidelines for commercial drone use. The bill, known as the Commercial UAS Modernization Act, would establish rules for commercial drones. The rules would govern the industry until FAA regulations are finalized.

Booker, a member of the Senate Subcommittee on Aviation Operations, Safety, and Security, has widely criticized the FAA's sluggish approach to the issue. In a statement reported by *Forbes* on May 12, 2015, Booker said the bill was meant to keep the United States from "falling further behind other countries because we lack rules for the safe operation of commercial UAS technology."

If passed, the law will create a deputy administrator position. The official would report to both the director of the FAA and the secretary of transportation. It also

THE ASSOCIATION FOR UNMANNED VEHICLE SYSTEMS INTERNATIONAL PREDICTS THAT 80 PERCENT OF THE COMMERCIAL DRONE MARKET BETWEEN 2015 AND 2025 WILL BE FOR AGRICULTURAL USES.

suggests that the FAA develop a test for licensing drone pilots. Like the regulations in effect at the time the bill was introduced, the new law would limit commercial drones to line-of-sight flights. However, it also allows exemptions and calls for officials to create regulations that let UAVs fly farther than that. In March 2016, the Senate Committee on Small Business and Entrepreneurship held hearings on the matter.

US Representative Michael C. Burgess, a Republican from Texas and chairman of the House Subcommittee on

Commerce, Manufacturing, and Trade, said in a statement in November 2015:

> *"American drone makers have shown their commitment to innovation in turning what was once seen as science fiction into a reality available to consumers and businesses across the country. There are many exciting drone applications in various stages of development. Entrepreneurship and innovation are part of this country's foundation, and we should be searching for ways to position the US as a leader in drone technology development."*

The United States still lags behind other countries in commercial drone use. But entrepreneurship and innovation may soon mean that UAV proliferation will force the hand of both business and government to accommodate it. Drones in commerce are here to stay, and will only become more important in the years and decades to come.

ADIT A horizontal mine entrance used for access, water drainage, or ventilation.

CROP YIELD The measurement, also called agricultural output, of the amount of grain produced per unit of land.

DRONE An unmanned aircraft that is remotely controlled by a person.

EXEMPTION Authorization to be free from a rule.

GEOPROBE A machine that drives steel rods into the ground to aid in taking samples below the land surface.

GIMBAL A device used to mount a camera onto a drone.

LINE-OF-SIGHT The distance within a person's view.

MINE RECLAMATION Returning land to a natural or usable state after mining operations end.

PRECISION AGRICULTURE An approach to farming that uses sophisticated data analysis to make management decisions.

PROTOTYPE An original model of a machine or other device used as a sample that can be copied or used to create future designs.

QUADCOPTER A helicopter drone with four rotors.

REMOTE CONTROLLED (RC) AIRCRAFT An aerial vehicle operated by a person on the ground using radio signals.

REMOTELY PILOTED VEHICLE (RPV) An unmanned aircraft piloted by a human pilot or piloting system not mounted on the vehicle.

RESOLUTION The amount of detail in a photographic image.

ROTOR A propeller such as those used on helicopters.

SPECTRAL SIGNATURE A measure of the electromagnetic energy reflected from an object compared with the amount of electromagnetic energy striking the object.

SPONTANEOUS COMBUSTION A way to start a fire of organic matter, like coal, by internally generating heat through loss of electrons by a molecule, atom, or ion.

TAILINGS POND A wet storage area for particles and chemicals left over from mining operations.

TILTROTOR A drone with rotors mounted on top of the craft so it can take off vertically. The rotors then tilt forward to transfer the job of lifting the drone to the wings.

UNMANNED AERIAL VEHICLE (UAV) An aircraft that navigates without a human pilot onboard.

FOR MORE INFORMATION

Association of Unmanned Vehicle Systems International (AUVSI)
2700 South Quincy Street, Suite 400
Arlington, VA 22206
(571) 255-7784
Website: http://www.auvsi.org/home
The Association for Unmanned Vehicle Systems International is a nonprofit organization
for advancing the unmanned systems and robotics community. Its more than 7,500
members support the use of drones in the defense, civil, and commercial sectors.

Canadian Centre for Unmanned Vehicle Systems (CCUVS)
#4, 49 Viscount Avenue SW
Medicine Hat, AB T1A 5G4
Canada
(403) 488-7208
Website: http://www.ccuvs.com
CCUVS is a nonprofit organization whose purpose is to facilitate sustained, profit-
able growth in the Canadian civil and commercial unmanned systems sector. Its
board of directors includes representatives from academia, industry, and
government who work primarily in the air unmanned systems environments.

Unmanned Aerial Vehicle Systems Association (UAVS)
Alexandra House
St John Street
Salisbury, Wiltshire SP1 2SB
United Kingdom
+44 (0) 1600 860193
Website: https://www.uavs.org
UAVS is the trade association for the United Kingdom's UAV industry, dedicated to
promoting its members and the unmanned aircraft systems industry's interests
through government lobbying efforts.

Unmanned Systems Canada
PO Box 81055
Ottawa ON K1P 1B1
Canada

(613) 526-5487
Website: https://www.unmannedsystems.ca
Unmanned Systems Canada promotes awareness, education, and appreciation
    of the unmanned vehicle systems community—including industry, academia,
    government, military, and others—in Canada and around the world.

Small UAV Coalition
1333 New Hampshire Avenue NW
Washington DC 200036
(202) 887-4043
Website: http://www.smalluavcoalition.org
The Small UAV Coalition works for changes in government policy and laws to allow
    the operation of small unmanned aerial vehicles (UAVs) beyond the line-of-sight,
    with varying degrees of autonomy, for commercial, consumer, recreational, and
    philanthropic purposes.

United States Association of Unmanned Aerial Videographers (UAVUS), Inc.
4880 Lower Roswell Road, Suite 165-505
Marietta, GA 30068
(770) 299-9602
Website: http://www.uavus.org/#section-8088
UAVUS is a professional association of civil and civic commercial UAV operators in
    the United States. It provides products and services to its members and works
    with federal, state, and local governments to develop policies and advocate for
    the use of UAVs in creating economic opportunities for commercial operators.

WEBSITES

Because of the changing nature of internet links, Rosen Publishing has developed
an online list of websites related to the subject of this book. This site is updated
regularly. Please use this link to access this list:

http://www.rosenlinks.com/IWD/comm

FOR FURTHER READING

Ambrosio, Donovan. *Domestic Drones: Elements and Considerations for the U.S.* Hauppauge, NY: Nova Science Publishers, 2014.

Baichtal, John. *Building Your Own Drones.* Indianapolis, IN: Que Publishing, 2015.

Brook, Henry. *Drones.* London, UK: Usborne Books, 2015.

Carey, Bill. *Enter the Drones.* Atglen, PA: Schiffer Publishing, 2016.

Collard, Sneed B. *Technology Forces: Drones and War Machines.* Vero Beach, FL: Rourke Educational Media, 2014.

Deans, John D. *Become a U.S. Commercial Drone Pilot.* North Vancouver, BC, Canada: Self-Counsel Press, 2016.

Gerdes, Louise I. *Drones.* Farmington Hills, MI: Greenhaven Press, 2014.

Greenhaven Press editors. *Drones.* Farmington Hills, MI: Greenhaven Press, 2016.

Dougherty, Martin. *Drones: An Illustrated Guide to the Unmanned Aircraft that Are Filling Our Skies.* London, UK: Amber Books, 2015.

Elliott, Alex. *Build Your Own Drone Manual.* Sparkford, UK: Haynes Publishing, 2016.

Juniper, Adam. *The Complete Guide to Drones.* London, UK: ILEX, 2015.

Kilby, Terry, and Belinda Kilby. *Getting Started with Drones.* Sebastopol, CA: Maker Media, 2015.

LaFay, Mark. *Drones for Dummies.* Hoboken, NJ: John Wiley & Sons Inc., 2015.

LeMieux, Jerry. *Drone Entrepreneurship.* Phoenix, AZ: Unmanned Vehicle University Press, 2013.

Make editors. *Drone Projects: A Collection of Drone-based Essays, Tutorials, and Projects.* Sebastopol, CA: Maker Media, 2016.

Masters, Nancy Robinson. *Drone Pilot.* North Mankato, MN: Cherry Lake Publishing, 2013.

Medea, Benjamin. *Drone Warfare.* Brooklyn, NY: Verso Books, 2013.

Miller, Michael. *The Internet of Things: How Smart TVs, Smart Cars, Smart Homes, and Smart Cities Are Changing the World.* Indianapolis, IN: Que Publishing, 2015.

Spillsbury, Louise. *Drones.* New York, NY: Gareth Stevens Publishing, 2016.

BIBLIOGRAPHY

Associated Press. "FAA to require most drones to be registered." *Finance and Commerce*, December 14, 2015. (http://finance-commerce.com/2015/12/faa-to-require-most-drones-to-be-registered/#ixzz40OMhK756).

Bloomberg News. "E-commerce Drone Delivery Could Take Off in a Few Years, a Google Exec Says." Internetretailer.com, January 11, 2016. (https://www.internetretailer.com/2016/01/11/google-e-commerce-drone-delivery-could-take-few-years).

Doering, Christopher. "Growing Use of Drones Poised to Transform Agriculture." *USA Today*, March 23, 2014. Retrieved March 16, 2016. (http://www.usatoday.com/story/money/business/2014/03/23/drones-agriculture-growth/6665561).

Droneblog. "Domicopter—Pizza Delivered by a Drone?" Retrieved February 2, 2016. (http://droneblog.co.uk/domicopter-pizza-delivered-by-a-drone).

DroneSkyPics.com "Google Might Have Drones Deliver Packages to Robots On Wheels." January 28, 2016. (http://droneskypics.com/google-might-have-drones-deliver-packages-to-robots-on-wheels-a-vision-for-safer-and-more-reliable-drone-deliveries).

Finding Dulcinea staff. "On This Day: Austria Drops Balloon Bombs on Venice." FindingDulcinea.com, August 22, 2011. (http://www.findingdulcinea.com/news/on-this-day/July-August-08/On-this-Day--Austria-Rains-Balloon-Bombs-on-Venice.html).

French, Sally. "How Drones will Drastically Transform U.S. Agriculture." Marketwatch.com, November 17, 2015. (http://www.marketwatch.com/story/how-drones-will-drastically-transform-us-agriculture-in-one-chart-2015-11-17).

Gunnilstam, Julius. "Amazon and Google Want Different Paths for Drones." USA Logistics, January 1, 2011. (http://www.ecomony.com/Amazon-and-Google-Want-Different-Paths-for-Drones,6945.html).

Kamran, Bilal. "Amazon Delivery Drones Facing Obstacles Amid Red Tape." Bidnessetc.com, January 19, 2016. (http://www.bidnessetc.com/61432-red-tape-keeps-amazon-from-flying-its-drones).

Mac, Ryan. "Senators Unveil Temporary Drone Laws That May Bode Well For Amazon and Google." Forbes, May 12, 2015. (http://www.forbes.com/sites/ryanmac/2015/05/12/commercial-drone-laws-cory-booker-john-hoeven-faa-google-amazon/#18bf2a35b502).

Martell, Allison. "Drone Miners for Survey Work." *Globe and Mail*, March 7, 2013. (http://www.theglobeandmail.com/report-on-business/industry-news/energy

-and-resources/drone-start-ups-woo-stretched-miners-for-survey-work
/article9467067).

Mehra, Gagan. "8 Obstacles to Drone Delivery, for Ecommerce." *Practical Commerce*, September 4, 2015. (http://www.practicalecommerce.com
/articles/91935-8-Obstacles-to-Drone-Delivery-for-Ecommerce).

Microdrones.com. "Air support in Open-cast Mining: New Perspectives in Raw Material Production Thanks to Drones." Retrieved February 17, 2016. (https://
www.microdrones.com/en/applications/growth-markets/drones-in-open-cast
-mining).

Moon, Mariella. "Amazon Exec Explains How Prime Air Delivery Drones Will Work." Engadet.com, February 3, 2016. (http://droneskypics.com/amazon-exec
-explains-how-prime-air-delivery-drones-will-work-vp-paul-misener-said
-prime-air-might-launch-outside-the-us-if-regulations-arent-ready-yet).

Morgan, David, and Allison Lampert. "Amazon Blasts FAA for Slowness on Drone Regulation." Recode, March 24, 2015. (http://recode.net/2015/03/24/amazon
-blasts-faa-for-slowness-on-drone-regulation).

Morgan, Tyne. "Agriculture Drone Business Takes Off." AgWeb.com, April 21, 2014. (http://www.agweb.com/article/agriculture_drone_business_takes_off_naa
_tyne_morgan).

Potter, Ben. "Drone-Buyer Checklist." AgWeb.com, March 21, 2014. (http://www
.agweb.com/article/drone-buyer_checklist_naa_ben_potter).

Potter, Ben. "Eight Ways to Employ Drones on the Farm." AgWeb.com, September 27, 2013. (http://www.agweb.com/article/eight_ways_to_employ_drones_on
_the_farm_naa_ben_potter-ben-potter).

Seidler, Kelsey. "Amazon Reveals Goals for Drones in E-Commerce Retailing." *LPM Insider*, January 20, 2016. (http://losspreventionmedia.com/insider/retail
-industry/amazon-reveals-goals-for-drones-in-e-commerce-retailing).

Shellborn, Kerry. "Drones are Ready for Takeoff in the Mining Industry." *Mining and Exploration*, February 2015. (http://www.miningandexploration.ca/technology
/article/drones_are_ready_for_takeoff_in_the_mining_industry).

Toor, Amar. "This Start-up is Using Drones to Deliver Medicine in Rwanda." *The Verge*, April 5, 2016. (http://www.theverge.com/2016/4/5/11367274
/zipline-drone-delivery-rwanda-medicine-blood).

INDEX

ABOUT THE AUTHOR

Mary-Lane Kamberg is a professional writer specializing in nonfiction for teens. She once had the time of her life on a sightseeing helicopter ride over Missouri's Ozark Mountains. Her husband, Ken, launched experimental drones for target practice when he was in the US Navy.

PHOTO CREDITS

Cover, p. 1 (drone) artpartner-images/Photographer's Choice/Getty Images; cover, p. 1 (background) Dusan Petkovic/Shutterstock.com; p. 5 Boris Horvat/AFP/Getty Images; p. 9 Hulton Archive/Hulton Fine Art Collection/Getty Images; p. 11 Friedrich Schmidt/Photographer's Choice/Getty Images; p. 14 Arctic-Images/Corbis Documentary/Getty Images; p. 18, 20, 21, 39, 46, 54 Bloomberg/Getty Images; p. 22 David Malan/Photographer's Choice RF/Getty Images; p. 26 George Rose/Getty Images; p. 28 AFP/Getty Images; p. 30 Cultura RM Exclusive/Joseph Giacomin/Getty Images; p. 34 Kletr/Shutterstock.com; p. 36 Chau Doan/LightRocket/Getty Images; p. 41 Frank Perry/AFP/Getty Images; p. 42 Sean Gallup/Getty Images; p. 49 David McNew/Getty Images; p. 51 Peter Cade/The Image Bank/Getty Images; cover and interior page backgrounds (geometric patterns) Sumkinn/Shutterstock.com; interior pages backgrounds (sky) Serg64/Shutterstock.com, (wave pattern) Kwirry/Shutterstock.com.

Designer: Brian Garvey; Editor/Photo Researcher: Philip Wolny